ILKLEY
REVISITED

MIKE DIXON

The
History
Press

Looking down-river towards the Old Bridge, *c.* 1907. The lane on the left is the original Nesfield Road, which in those days stayed close to the river bank after leaving the Old Bridge. (T. Mutton)

First published 2010

The History Press
The Mill, Brimscombe Port
Stroud, Gloucestershire, GL5 2QG
www.thehistorypress.co.uk

© Mike Dixon, 2010

The right of Mike Dixon to be identified as the Author
of this work has been asserted in accordance with the
Copyrights, Designs and Patents Act 1988.

ISBN 978 0 7524 4894 7

Typesetting and origination by The History Press
Printed and bound in India by Replika Press Pvt. Ltd.
Manufacturing managed by Jellyfish Print Solutions Ltd

CONTENTS

ACKNOWLEDGEMENTS

I am very grateful to the collectors of Ilkley photographs who have given me access to their collections; to the late Gordon Burton and his wife Betty, Tim Mutton, Win Porritt, and the late Dorothy Craven, and to many other individuals credited in the captions who have contributed photographs. I owe a particular debt to Jack Tipping, who gave me a comprehensive set of old Ilkley postcards collected by his father and which have formed the starting point for my own, now extensive, collection.

Special thanks are due to those who have photographed the passing scene and who have loaned items from their collections, in particular F.W. (Bill) Smith, Michael Grunwell, and Anthony Thornton, and to those stalwarts who took the photographs for the *Ilkley Gazette* and other publications that are reproduced herein.

I am indebted to Mel Vasey, the former editor of the *Ilkley Gazette*, for access to the newspaper's archives and permission to reproduce photographs, and to Paul Langan and Tina Tipping for facilitating that access; thanks to Geoffrey de Vere and Joan Duncan for passing on photographs taken by the late C. Millar Duncan; to Elizabeth Lepelley for photographs; and to Derek Breare for helpful information relating to Ilkley garages; to Gavin Edwards at the Manor House Art Gallery and Museum for access to photographs; to Barry Rennison of the Samuel Ledgard Society; to Andrew Walbank and Graham Peacock for photographs and information about Scouting in Ilkley; and to Paul Bourgeois for photographs relating to the Black Hats versus White Hats cricket matches and for his help in identifying many of the vintage cars that decorate the street scenes in this book. Thanks are due to May Pickles who gave me access to the Ilkley scrapbooks collected by the late Kate Mason. These proved to be an invaluable resource.

Others have willingly shared their knowledge of 'old Ilkley' events and characters and I wish to thank Jack and Joyce Tipping, Shirley Watson, Shannon Houliston and Andrew Sharpe, for many enlightening and amusing conversations.

Finally, I wish to thank Judy, my wife, for introducing me to Ilkley and for our fifty years collecting memories together.

INTRODUCTION

It is ten years since my first compilation of old Ilkley photographs was published. Mine was not the first, however, and in the meantime other collections have appeared, so the need for another book of photographs could be questioned. I suggest there are three reasons why a new book is entirely justified.

Firstly, the previous works have concentrated on buildings and the changing townscape. I felt there was a need for a new collection that had as its primary objective people and events. Secondly, my perspective on what constitutes popular history has changed. I am passionately interested in the Victorian period, but I appreciate that others find it much easier to identify with the twentieth century. Indeed, photographs that evoke childhood memories or bring to mind recollections they have heard from their grandparents, are much more likely to give pleasure through shared nostalgia. But how old must a photograph be to qualify as 'historic'? I take the view that photographs are historic if they record an event or a way of life that has passed, as are those that capture the passing scene. Our towns change so rapidly in terms of shops, transport, demolition and reconstruction, that even recent photographs can have historical validity. Aspects of 'disappearing Ilkley', some major, others minor, are well represented in this book.

The third motive behind this new compilation is a desire to present the reader with previously unpublished photographs. A succession of illustrated books (and booklets) on Ilkley history have at their core a relatively small series of Victorian photographs taken from old postcards that have been reproduced in various combinations in all of them. I have endeavoured to exclude any illustration that has been reproduced elsewhere, although in providing over 230 'new' images I may not have succeeded completely.

Old Ilkley guidebooks have provided some of these images. Under the title 'The Heather Spa', the guides sought to attract visitors to this inland resort. They extolled the virtues of moorland air, country walks and riverside scenery, but also lay emphasis on the varied entertainments, the sporting facilities and the physical attractions of the town. The opening chapter recapitulates this approach.

Over the years photographers have captured people at work and play. A particular group of people that have kept us entertained over the years are the Ilkley Players. They, and other amateur theatricals, perform through these pages. Sport also provides workers with playtime, but a particular sporting event receives special attention. The annual novelty cricket match played by Ilkley tradesmen and, latterly, tradeswomen – the Black Hats versus White Hats match, has given rise to a photographic feast. The fun and frolics surrounding the event paved the way for the town's charity carnival, which quite soon came to have a separate existence that has also been well documented through the years.

People are at the fore in chapter six 'Serving the Community'. Soldiers, nurses and first-aid volunteers remind us of wartime service, but here they rub shoulders with Scouts and Guides, with hospital staff and workers in our convalescent homes, people who have strengthened the peace in our community.

Transport and the changing fabric of the town are recorded, but I have endeavoured to enliven the images with mention of the people involved. The church-goers and schoolchildren, the railwaymen and garage owners, and the man who kept the donkeys that transported visitors up to White Wells, all these populate the book.

The town's ever-changing shops in Brook Street and Leeds Road are seen at particular moments in time, while The Grove displays its essential character over the years – a street for shopping and for promenading.

Finally, natural events have provided many fascinating images. Ilkley is prone to flooding; periods of intense rainfall higher up Wharfedale can result in the river bursting its banks, or, as happened most notably in 1900, rain of monsoon proportions falling on Ilkley Moor can convert normally docile streams into torrents that produce flash-floods and subsequent destruction of property. The disruptive and, for some, pleasurable aspects of heavy snow-falls on the town have also been recorded by our intrepid photographers.

Through the events, both natural and man-made, and the people represented in these pages, I hope I have successfully encompassed the passing years and the spirit of the times – the social history of Ilkley. There are colourful characters leaping from these monochrome images but there are also plenty of good 'ordinary' folk who have populated the history of this extraordinary town. You might be one of them!

Mike Dixon, 2010

1

THE HEATHER SPA

Down by the Old Bridge, *c.* 1890. No boating today. Following a prolonged dry spell, people are able to stroll over the pebbles in the river bed. The ladies on the bank have set aside their umbrellas, currently being used as parasols, and one of them is apparently observing the gentlemen through a telescope. (G. Burton)

The Old Bridge, *c.* 1950. The iconic bridge, rebuilt after the disastrous Wharfedale flood of 1673, has been closed to vehicular traffic since the 1930s. Despite conspicuous notices, however, cars were regularly driven across the bridge – particularly by the occupants of Stubham Rise. The ban on cars was so regularly ignored that eventually the Council erected bollards across both ends. Now only bicycles, horses and (illegally) motorbikes can be ridden across. Here a couple linger on the bridge but the distant view down-river reveals something of a blot on the landscape – the gas-works retort house. (M. Dixon)

Fishing at Ilkley, 1893. The unidentified angler is fly fishing close to the 'Crum Wheel Bend' of the river. Denton Road runs along the left-hand bank. Nowadays the view down-river would be obscured by the suspension bridge (built 1934). The fishing rights for this stretch of the Wharfe are owned by the Ilkley Angling Club, which replenishes the stocks of brown trout. Although the scene appears tranquil, when the river is in spate this can be a dangerous spot. (M. Dixon)

Mr Dell's rowing boats, *c.* 1935. In April or May each year, Mr Dell would pay some of the local lads 2 or 3p to move large stones from the river bed that had been brought down by the winter flow, and use them to create a dam. In this way a shallow pool was formed suitable for rowing boats. The lads could earn a similar amount after every flood for rebuilding the dam. Onlookers crowd the river bank to watch the rowers come and go from the landing stage. (C.M. Duncan)

On the Wharfe, *c.* 1935. Young rowers get set for a race down the river. (C.M. Duncan)

Left: An otter hunt, *c.* 1938. The Kendal and District otter hounds regularly visited the Wharfe near Ilkley to hunt otters. Here the huntsmen are looking for otter pad marks in the sand – rather difficult amongst the dog and human footprints! The hounds themselves require no visual evidence; using their highly developed sense of smell they can detect the scent of an otter up to twenty-four hours after it has passed through the place. (C.M. Duncan)

Below: Otter hounds in the Wharfe, *c.* 1938. The huntsman shouts 'Try down' and the pack head downstream. Hunting otters was banned in 1978 and so the Kendal pack is no more. Indeed otter hounds are a rare breed, with less than 1,000 worldwide – about twice as rare as the giant panda! (C.M. Duncan)

Right: The stepping stones, *c.* 1906. The stepping stones across the Wharfe in Ben Rhydding were another aspect of the Heather Spa that evoked 'Sweet Memories' – but possibly only when the river was low! The stones are situated near Wheatley Lane and allow the intrepid walker to cross to the north side of the river near Carters Lane. (Shirley Wise)

Below: Wells House and the 'White Wells' filter house, *c.* 1898. Perhaps the most prestigious of the hydropathic establishments in Ilkley, Wells House is seen here in its fully developed state, with the Winter Gardens and Annexe to the right of the main building. In the middle ground, the newly-built filter house used a novel system of pressurized filtration to purify the water from the Panorama and Hill Top Reservoirs before distribution into the town's water mains. Note the almost complete lack of housing on the Middleton side of the river. (M. Dixon)

The Tarn, *c*. 1898. Opened in 1875, the Tarn, with its surrounding 'promenade', rapidly established itself as one of the town's attractions. Created from Craig Dam, a man-made pond that provided an additional water supply to the corn mills at the top of Mill Ghyll, the construction of the Tarn was financed by public subscription. Note that three islands were present at this time; the nearest had a fountain fed by gravity from a small reservoir up the hillside. (M. Dixon)

The Tarn, July 1904. Crowds assemble around the makeshift bandstand on the south side of the Tarn for 'Infirmary Sunday'. The holding of open-air concerts to raise funds for hospitals was common throughout Yorkshire, but this was the first such event in Ilkley. Thanks to the initiative of the Ilkley Orpheus Glee Union, 'a most successful musical service in aid of the Leeds Infirmary' took place on 17 July. The concert raised £19, a seemingly poor return but worth about 100 times as much in today's values. (M. Dixon)

Cooper's Tarn Pierrots, 1906. The moustachioed gentleman is the celebrated Mr Christopher Cooper. At the time he was landlord of the North View Hotel, opposite the station, but he was a man with strong theatrical connections. His wife's father was Henry Pullan, who opened the great 3,000-seat Theatre of Varieties in Brunswick Place, Bradford, in 1869. Pullan's Music Hall became nationally famous and such stars as the comedian Dan Leno and the tight-rope walker Blondin ('The Hero of Niagara') appeared there. Christopher Cooper became the theatre manager there before moving into the hotel trade when the theatre closed. (T. Mutton)

The bandstand, c. 1916. By 1900 Ilkley had a splendid brass band (thanks to the purchase of all the instruments from the trustees of Calverley Brass Band for £42 in 1899) but the band had nowhere to play. In 1904 a bandstand was erected in West View Park (now the site of the car park below Darwin Gardens) at a cost of £120 and, at least in the summer months, the band had a suitable 'home'. In the following year, a covered seating area was provided so that the band would still have an audience in bad weather. After completion of the Winter Gardens in 1913, the weather became less important as the bands now had an alternative, all-weather venue. Performances continued until the 1930s and the bandstand survived until after the war. Then, unused, forlorn and increasingly vandalised, it was demolished in the late 1940s. (M. Dixon)

White Wells and the Tea Rooms, 1950s. The Tea Rooms were a seasonal amenity. During the summer months, Mrs Wilkinson would come up from her home in Chantry Drive and serve refreshments at the chalet. Despite its distance from the town it did have a mains gas supply and the premises were lit by gas mantles. In those days there was also a sweet shop in the top end of White Wells – accessed by the steps at the rear. After repeated episodes of vandalism the Council decided to demolish the Tea Rooms in the late 1960s. (M. Dixon)

The paddling pool and Wells Terrace in the1950s. The pool was created in the 1920s from a pre-existing pond, Hainsworth's Pond, made many years before by damming one of the streams coming down from the moor. Wells Terrace was erected by Marshall Hainsworth in 1857. He and his family occupied one of the houses while the other two were let. The building's main claim to fame is that Charles Darwin and his family stayed here in the autumn of 1859 at the time of publication of *On the Origin of Species*. Many Ilkley residents will be more familiar with its period as St Winifred's Maternity Hospital, from where they will date their own origins. (M. Dixon)

The Grove Picture House, 1967. The building, originally a lecture hall, was opened as a cinema by the Croft Brothers in 1913. The brothers had other interests in the town, and James Croft continued as a coal merchant into the 1930s. After the war, the cinema was bought by the Star Group. The cinema was unusual in having a row of double-seats down each side. These were, of course, in great demand by courting couples. The current showing, and one of the last films to be shown here, is *The Greatest Story Ever Told*, starring Max von Sydow as Jesus. The cinema was demolished in 1968. (C.M. Duncan)

Essoldo cinema, 1968. Built as the 'New Cinema' in 1928, it became the Essoldo after the Second World War. The cinema could seat 1,050 people, and the building contained a large ballroom ('dance-hall' to the locals) and two shops. On the right is the entrance to the dance hall, while down the right-hand side was another entrance with its own cashier's box giving access to the 'cheap seats' at the front of the cinema. The commissionaire had to watch out for kids coming in at the cheap end who would then crawl under the seats and emerge in the more expensive seats at the back, and had to be escorted by torchlight back to their proper places! The cinema closed in 1969, the final offering being *The Italian Job* starring Michael Caine, Noel Coward and Benny Hill. (P.A. Thornton)

The sports fields, *c.* 1959. The riverside meadows or 'holmes' provided the ideal location for sports fields. In the foreground is the car park adjacent to the open-air swimming pool – the indoor pool did not appear until 1974, but at least the pool was heated in those days. The gas heating plant for the pool was housed in the building on the right. Beyond are tennis courts and the ground of the Ilkley Cricket Club (which moved here from the Railway Road ground in 1898). Across Denton Road are the grandstand (built 1924), clubhouse (1937) and pitches of Ilkley Rugby Club (founded 1879). (A. Anning/M. Dixon)

Cricket at Ilkley, *c.* 1936. The Craven Gentlemen, a long-established 'wandering' cricket club, opened their 1936 season on the Ilkley ground by beating Durham University by 3 wickets. They had an illustrious history and a prestigious fixture list including matches against university teams, major public schools, and even an annual match at Gargrave against the Craven Ladies. These are the players who beat Durham University: From left to right, front row: T. Crowther, H.B. Dawson, Revd C.E.D. Crane (President), J.F. Best, H.P. Shackleton. Back row: R.A.F. James, A.G. Gaunt, E.C. Polter, C.S. Moxon, H.S. Scott, J.W. Lawton. H. Wood, C.B. Atkinson. (*Ilkley Gazette*)

The swimming pool, *c.* 1950. A sustained period of warm weather brought crowds of people to the pool. There are far more poolside spectators and sunbathers on the grass than swimmers, but they couldn't all swim at once! The retort house of the gasworks dominates the view of the town behind. In those days the pool was open from 9 a.m. until 9 p.m. each day; in the evenings the whole area was illuminated by 'fairy lights' that gave the scene a magical quality. (A. Anning/M. Dixon)

The swimming pool, *c.* 1936. The outdoor bathing pool was opened in 1935 and became an instant success. A public outdoor pool was a great novelty in Yorkshire and people came from far and wide to take a dip. The pool was built by Ilkley Council but its running was handed over to the caterers, Taylors of Harrogate; their small café is seen behind. This was a great place to while away the time. It was surrounded by a glass-screen that acted as a wind-break as well as providing a splendid observation post. Waitresses in smart black-and-white uniforms plied between the tables and the tea came in silver pots. A highlight of a day at the pool was to order a 'ham salad tea' costing *2s 6d* all in. (T. Mutton)

Moor Golf Club House, *c.* 1920. Ilkley's first golf course was opened in 1890 on the edge of Ilkley Moor, just off the Keighley Gate Road. When, in 1894, the Local Board demanded a large increase in rent to renew the lease, the club decided to move to a new course down by the river, taking their pavilion with them! The moor course was handed over to a group of tradesmen who formed the Olicana Golf Club. In 1899, they struck a deal with the Council whereby the UDC undertook the management of the moor links and appointed an attendant to supervise the playing arrangements at a cost of 10s 6d per member. The name was changed to the Ilkley Moor Golf Club and a replacement club house was opened in 1907. The club remained in existence until the 1940s. (M. Dixon)

Ilkley Golf Club House, *c.* 1920. The riverside course was formally opened in 1898 by the Hon. Secretary Mr A.W. Godby. While the nucleus of the clubhouse was the building transferred from the moor; it was doubled in size when it was re-erected. Its new location, however, was remote from any mains services. A spring on the site was utilised for the water supply and an acetylene gas plant was installed to provide heating and lighting. Electricity didn't arrive until 1928. (M. Dixon)

Teeing off, *c.* 1939. Gentlemen (with their caddies) playing on the riverside course at Ilkley. The light dusting of snow made putting even trickier than usual. (C.M. Duncan)

The view from the club house, 1940s. The veranda was a favourite place for players who had finished their rounds to take refreshment and look down on the 18th fairway. On occasions, players who had taken a lot of refreshment would challenge each other to drive a ball from the flat area at the top of the steps leading to the veranda, to the other side of the river. Although this would take a mighty hit, the river was closer to the clubhouse in those days and there were far fewer trees! (Anning/*Ilkley Gazette*)

Above: Airedale Beagles at the Tarn, *c.* 1951. Beagling is the hunting of hares on foot with a pack of hounds. The followers of the hunt were also on foot, and they went up hill and down dale trying to keep up with the hounds. One long-time follower was asked what they did with the hare when they caught it. He replied that he didn't know – he had never seen them catch one! The Airedale Beagles was formed after the chance meeting of Tom Clarke and Dawson Jowett on Ilkley Moor in 1891. Tom became the kennel-man and Dawson the huntsman, a position that he held for forty-two years. (A. Anning/M. Dixon)

Left: An Airedale Beagles 'trophy'. This mounted hare's head proves that the hunt did occasionally catch its quarry. This hare was caught on 19 December 1936 and is identified as 'Royality' [*sic*]. Presumably the hunt started at the Royalty pub at Otley Chevin. The stuffed head now hangs on a wall at the Falcon Inn in Arncliffe, Littondale. (M. Dixon)

Stack's Field, March 1966. A match in progress during the Ilkley Rugby Union seven-a-side tournament, one of the premier schools rugby tournaments in the north of England. In 1966 the competition was won for the first time by Hemsworth Grammar School from South Yorkshire. In the 1980s the tournament went into a decline as junior rugby moved away from its school base towards the rugby clubs. (*Ilkley Gazette*)

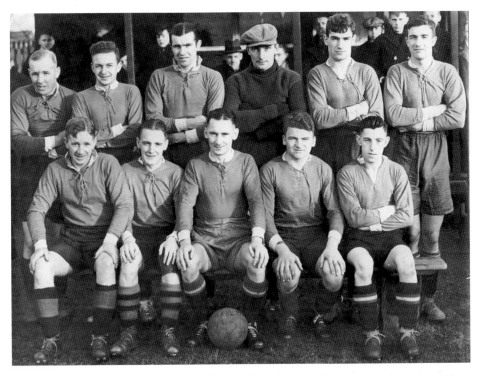

Football at Ilkley, January 1936. The semi-final of the Wharfedale League Cup was played at Ilkley. Unfortunately, the local team, Addingham FC, was beaten by Horsforth Hotspurs. The members of the losing Addingham team are seen here posing before the match. From left to right, back row: Herbert Holmes, George Hanson, K. Lowe, S. Hewdle, T. Walmsley, ? Walmsley. Front row: Edgar Holmes, L. Booth, S. Fisher (captain), H. Gell, T. Wilson. In those days a cloth cap was the universal headgear worn by goalkeepers; this is not a peculiarity of the Addingham 'custodian'. (*Ilkley Gazette*)

Above: Ilkley Lawn Tennis Club, *c.* 1939. The annual Open Tennis tournament is in full swing. The tournament had been held every year (apart from during the First World War) at the August bank-holiday weekend for over fifty years. Looking across the river, the large house on the right is 'Goodwood', demolished to make way for a housing development in the 1970s. (M. Dixon)

Left: Jumping off the Calf Rock, *c.* 1938. (A. Anning/M. Dixon)

2

BY ROAD, RAIL
... AND DONKEY

Wells House Garage, *c.* 1938. W.H. Hutchinson was originally the manager of the stables at Wells House Hotel and lived in Ivy Lodge, one of the two houses astride the entrance of the stable yard. In 1912 Hutchinson, with financial support from the photographer William Scott, established a garage in Middleton Road. For some years, Hutchinson ran the garage in tandem with the livery stables at Wells House, but after the First World War, with the decline in horse transport, he converted the stables into a second garage business. During the Second World War, the Wells House Garage was requisitioned by the War Department and used by the Officer Training Corps based in Ilkley. Lorries and other military vehicles were parked in the former stable yard, necessitating sentries on permanent 'watch' at the front. (D. Craven)

Motor Cars and Cycles completely
overhauled, tuned up. etc

———

STOCKS ALL BEST MAKES.

Oils, Tyres, Petrol, Benzol and Motor
Accessories.

AUSTIN HARRISON,

AUTOMOBILE ENGINEER,

51, Brook Street, Ilkley.

═══

The Most Central Garage.

Above: W.H. Hutchinson & Co., Middleton
Garage, *c.* 1914. The garage, which had
a large workshop and multiple individual
garages behind, was entered through the
square archway behind the first car. The
car on the extreme left is a Lanchester
from around 1907. The car turning
onto the road is a Simplex, a luxury car
made in Sheffield, and the car in the
foreground is a Fiat from around 1912.
Mr Hutchinson employed four other
mechanics at the Middleton Road Garage
at this time. (D. Craven)

Left: An advertisement for Austin
Harrison, automobile engineer, *c.* 1920.
Ilkley's first motor repair and maintenance
shop was founded around 1907 when
Fred Heap & Co. was taken over by John
F. Wainwright, who changed the business
from pianos and cycles to automobiles.
Wainwright's so-called Grove Garage was
thus a shop at 10 The Grove. Here we
have another shop-based 'garage' run
by a pioneer automobile engineer whose
parents had the considerable foresight to
name him 'Austin'. (M. Dixon)

Cunnington's boot and shoe repair shop in Railway Road, *c.* 1935. After the First World War, Harold Tunnicliffe built this hut using his gratuity from the army and started a motorcar repair business. Harold married a local girl, Olive Glover, and in 1923 went into partnership with her brother Harry, a former railway worker, and the partners moved into larger premises. Thereafter, Tom Cunnington, who lived in Nelson Road, purchased the hut and remained there until the Second World War. (Elizabeth Lepelley)

The Old Barn at Wood Rhydding, Skipton Road, *c.* 1936. This building provided the 'larger premises' in which Messrs Tunnicliffe and Glover established their first garage. 'Wood Rhydding' was the name given to the cluster of houses at the western edge of Ilkley (together with Hadfield's farm), which in the nineteenth century were almost a separate hamlet. The barn has been converted into a house and still stands today, back from the main road. (E. Lepelley)

Tunnicliffe's Garage, Skipton Road, *c. 1938.* In 1932 the Tunnicliffe-Glover partnership was dissolved and Harry Glover took over the lease of the Bridge Lane Garage. Harold Tunnicliffe remained at Wood Rhydding until 1937, when he erected this purpose-built garage on land adjacent to the Lister's Arms Hotel. Among the mechanics at Tunnicliffe's was the genial Mr George Pennock, a popular man who was heavily involved with music in the town and ran the boy scout troop at All Saints' Church. (E. Lepelley)

Bridge Lane, 1962. The Bridge Lane garage was opened in 1917 by Alfred Wilkinson, who was the owner and head mechanic until 1932. In that year Harry Glover rented the building from him and Wilkinson withdrew from the garage to pursue his interest in electrical engineering. This was Glover's first garage in the town. The AA motorcycle and sidecar represent the final version then in use by the 'roadside' patrols. In 1963 they were replaced by small vans. (*Ilkley Gazette*)

Glovers Garage, Skipton Road, 1959. Charles Thackray purchased the former Wesleyan Chapel and museum from the Council and converted the building into a garage (Central Garage) in 1913. During the First World War, Mr Thackray served overseas with the army, and his wife managed the garage. During the 1930s, Thackray maintained cars previously owned by several celebrities including Ramon Navarro – a 'Latin Lover' from the silent movies, and Carl Brisson, a Danish film actor. The garage also serviced a Hispano Suiza limousine that had belonged to King Alfonso of Spain but was then owned by Mr Clough, owner of the New Cinema in Railway Road. In 1937 the garage was sold to Harry Glover. (D.R. Powell/*Ilkley Gazette*)

Station Garage, Springs Lane, *c.* 1990. This garage traded as Helliwell and Hobbs; 'Old Man' Helliwell exercised a managerial role and strode around the premises in a brown overall and trilby hat, while Mr Hobbs acted as chief mechanic in the workshop. After several changes of ownership, the garage was sold in the late 1990s to property developers and subsequently demolished. The site was purchased by McCarthy and Stone, who built retirement apartments, Carnegie Court, which were opened in 1999. (E. Lepelley)

ROSS BROTHERS
Limited.

THE MAIN AGENTS
FOR
AUSTIN - WOLSELEY - HUMBER
OLDSMOBILE - RILEY - FIAT
ARMSTRONG-SIDDELEY

Demonstrations at your Convenience

ROSS BROTHERS LTD
"SERVICE" BEN RHYDDING
RIVERSIDE, BEN RHYDDING. 'Phone Ilkley 1030
New & Used Car Showrooms : Wharfe View Rd., Ilkley. 'Phone Ilkley 10.

Deferred Terms Arranged

Left: An advertisement for Ross Brothers' Garage, *c.* 1937. (M. Dixon)

Below: Staff outing from Ross Brothers' Garage, *c.* 1950. The new and used car showroom was in Wharfe View Road, opposite the old All Saints' School. The lady standing next to the three men on the right of the group was Miss Lily Fish. According to some accounts, Miss Fish essentially ran Ross Bros. She was termed 'the Secretary' but in reality she did the books, looked after personnel, and ran the office. The men simply sold and maintained the cars! This building was originally erected before the Second World War for Charles Thackray. It was used as a school canteen during the war. (Betty Burton)

The Highfield Hotel (now the Cow and Calf) with a 'Moor Top' service bus waiting to take passengers back to the town centre. The near part of the building, which is right on the roadside, was an extension to the original hotel built in the 1890s. In recent years it was removed to give access to the rear car park. In the past, the hotel had a somewhat chequered career. Apart from the summer months when it was served by the bus service, it was rather inaccessible for most people. (P.A. Thornton)

A Ledgard bus at the New Brook Street terminus in April 1956. Samuel Ledgard (1874-1952) was a well-known local bus operator. His company ran services from Ilkley to Leeds via Guiseley (commencing in 1927 when they took over from the Frenchman, Jules Sylvian Antichan of Burley in Wharfedale) and from Ilkley to Otley (starting in 1932, a service originally operated by the Cream Bus Service of Burley in Wharfedale). A service linking Ilkley with Middleton Hospital commenced in November 1942. The queue for the Leeds bus was often a lengthy affair; some would use the waiting time to eat fish and chips purchased at Thornton's shop just up from the bus shelter. (J. Fozard/Samuel Ledgard Society Archive)

Staff at Ilkley railway station assembled on Platform 1, *c.* 1925. Tom Britton stands in the middle of the back row. Tom and his family lived in the railway cottages – Railway Terrace – running alongside Springs Lane. The railway company offered their employees a tied cottage when they were about to 'start a family'. Tom rose 'through the ranks' at Ilkley and ended up in charge of the Parcels Office at Bradford Exchange station. (Bradford Galleries and Museums)

The goods sidings, 1963. On the left are the platform and pens of the old cattle dock. The water tower on Platform 1 was not required for much longer, as steam made way for diesel during the early 1960s. (P.A. Thornton)

A steam goods train heads for Leeds, 1963. The train is passing the old part of Spooner Engineering, a building that was formerly the Ilkley Brewery. The photograph is taken from the old goods yard. (P.A. Thornton)

Ilkley station, c. 1964. Bank Holiday crowds wait on Platform 4 for a train to Leeds or Bradford from Skipton via Bolton Abbey. The train would no doubt already be crowded when it arrived in Ilkley as a trip to Bolton Abbey was a popular Bank Holiday excursion. Train services from Skipton were discontinued in March 1965. (F.W. Smith collection)

Ben Rhydding station, 1966. The station was erected in 1871 at the instigation of Ben Rhydding Hydro; there would have been no other reason for the rail company to build a station to serve the tiny hamlet of Wheatley. Thereafter the name of the station gradually began to be associated with the local area so that towards the end of the nineteenth century the village itself became known as Ben Rhydding. The original station was a small wooden structure, but Dr McLeod, the owner of Ben Rhydding Hydro, considered this inappropriate and spent £200 having this stone building erected. (F.W. Smith)

Ben Rhydding station, c. 1957. A passenger train heads for Bradford. (F.W. Smith collection)

Ilkley Railway Supporter's Association, *c.* 1964. Following Dr Beeching's proposed closure of the Wharfedale rail services, a group of local activists got together to try and save the line. At this meeting they are making their preparations for a hearing of the Transport Users Consultative Committee. The table is covered in letters of objection sent to the group. The chairman, Mr Hedley Wright, was a Bradford solicitor who had never taken a driving test so he was an unusually committed rail user. His wife drove the family car with one or more of their seven children on board, and ferried Hedley between meetings. The protest group were successful in keeping the line to Ilkley open, but not the services to Addingham, Bolton Abbey and Skipton. (*Ilkley Gazette*)

Ilkley station, *c.* 1971. The Skipton bus leaves the 'transport interchange', then situated in the forecourt. The former cab-man's shelter (now a waiting room at Embsay station, having been transplanted there in 1973) stands on the left of the exit. The shelter lay empty for many years. It is claimed that as a young man, the entertainer Jimmy Savile slept here for one night, having missed the last bus to Leeds. (P. Bambridge/*Ilkley Gazette*)

The viaduct over Bolton Bridge Road. This was demolished in 1973. (F.W. Smith)

The railway bridge across Easby Drive looking north, *c.* 1960. (P.A. Thornton)

A view of the railway bridge across Victoria Avenue looking north, *c.* 1960. Both bridges were removed in the first wave of demolition in 1967 following closure of the line. (P.A. Thornton)

A view of the railway bridge across the A65 looking back towards Ilkley, *c.* 1960. This bridge was demolished in 1967. At the same time the opportunity was taken to straighten the road. (P.A. Thornton)

Left: Mr Jackson outside his cottage in Bridge Lane, *c.* 1890. No book of old Ilkley images would be complete without a photograph of John 'Donkey' Jackson. A wool-comber by trade, John Jackson purchased the donkey business from William Rigg in 1868. He then ran this homely transport system until 1906, when he retired at the age of eighty. He died the following year. (G. Burton)

Below: Bridge Lane, *c.* 1870. 'Donkey' Jackson's cottage is pictured after the demolition of William Rigg's house next door. Thirty years later, Jackson's cottage was to undergo the same fate. The roof fell in and it had to be demolished. Jackson and his wife moved into Castle Yard, where he carried on his business for another six years. The steps leading up to his cottage are still in place in Bridge Lane. (G. Burton)

A FAMILI A FAMILIAR FIGURE.
ILKLEY.

3

FLOOD, SNOW AND ICE

The disastrous flood at Ilkley on Thursday, 12 July 1900, wrecked this house in Back Middleton Road. The *Ilkley Gazette* reported that; 'A thunderstorm of extraordinary severity was the first indication of coming disaster, accompanied by two hours' heavy and persistent downpour of rain, which in a very short time converted the four streams flowing through the town from the Moor into fierce raging torrents, causing loss of life and destruction of much valuable property of all kinds, from the demolition of business premises, houses and bridges, downwards. The damage is variously estimated at figures ranging from £50,000 to £70,000. In its destructive effects, the flood is believed to be unparalleled in the history of the valley.' (M. Dixon)

Left: The flood also caused the collapse of Mr Robert Brogden's coach-building workshop near Chapel Lane. Mr Brogden was away from Ilkley at the time – he was on the St Margaret's choir trip, but his three sons (Edward, Alfred and Robert Jr) were in the building together with the blacksmith Daniel Daugherty. As soon as the first crash was heard, Edward, Robert and Daniel evacuated the building, but Alfred, who was working upstairs, was trapped by the collapse of the roof and killed. His body was retrieved by the police some two hours after the roof collapse. (G. Burton)

Below: A general view of Mr Brogden's workshop after the flood. (M. Dixon)

A crowd watches water flooding from The Grove into Cunliffe Road, 1900. On the right, on the corner of Back Regent Road, is Heaps Pianos and Cycles (now Morten's 'top' shop). The hanging sign advertises Humber & Co. of Coventry, a major bicycle manufacturer of the day, but a company that became much better known as a maker of cars. The large house seen through the trees was later occupied for many years by Dr Jack Armstrong. (G. Burton)

Brook Street on the morning after the storm. (M. Dixon)

The scene outside the newly erected entrance to Septimus Wray's pleasure gardens in Bridge Lane. (M. Dixon)

St James's Road covered in rubble after the flood. (M. Dixon)

Shops in Church Street after the flood. There is an appeal on the barrel for donations to help Mr Brogden's widow. (M. Dixon)

The River Wharfe in flood at the New Bridge, 1906. The bridge had only recently been completed and surplus masonry can be seen scattered behind the fences marking the junction of Castle Road and New Brook Street. It was officially opened in June 1906 by Councillor J.A. Middlebrook, manager and secretary to the Ilkley Brewery and Aerated Water Co. (T. Mutton)

The Wharfe bursts its banks, Saturday, 16 February 1935. After days of torrential rain, the river rose over 10ft above its normal level and overflowed earlier that morning. (Bradford Galleries and Museums)

Looking across the flooded valley towards Nell Bank, 16 February 1935. At this time, the Misses Morley occupied the house at Nell Bank while in the grounds were livery and riding stables run by Bertram Eglen, who formerly had a riding school in the Old Brewery yard in Railway Road. After the war, the owner applied to build houses in the grounds but was refused planning permission. As a consequence the property was sold to Bradford Council and the house was subsequently demolished. In 1977 an outdoor educational centre for young people was opened on the site. (A. Anning/M. Dixon)

Rescuing passengers from three marooned buses on the A65 near Esscroft (Manor Park bends), 16 February 1935. The road was flooded for several miles between Ilkley and Otley. The stranded vehicle is an Albion pick-up truck. (A. Anning/M. Dixon)

One horse power, 16 February 1935. A van is towed through the floodwater on Denton Road, just opposite Ben Rhydding bridge. The roadway across the bridge was under a foot of water. The van, a seven-horse-power Jowett, belonged to Johnson's Café Royal ('High Class Confectioners and Bakers') in Brook Street. (C.M. Duncan)

Left: The Old Bridge, 1936. On this Monday morning, the Wharfe is in an angry mood after a weekend in which previous heavy snow thawed at the same time as heavy rain fell higher up the dale. The building in the background is the Middelton Hotel (later the Ilkley Moor Hotel). (C.M. Duncan)

Below: Golfers on the 18th green at the Ilkley Golf Club course, 1936. The course was flooded for the second weekend running after a rapid thaw and torrential rain. The golfers managed a 'part-round' and, despite the abundant 'casual water' and high wind, declared that they had enjoyed themselves. Such is the fortitude of the keen golfer. (C.M. Duncan)

The Old Bridge in the snow, 1900. (M. Dixon)

A snowy morning in Skipton Road, 1906. The sweepers are clearing the pavement outside the town's first museum. The museum was funded by private donations and created from the former Wesleyan Chapel at the corner of Bolton Bridge Road (now part of Nidd Vale Motors). The Revd Robert Collyer opened the museum in 1892. It was a short-lived affair however, as in 1908 the collection was transferred to the newly-opened library building. (M. Dixon)

Church Street in the snow, *c*. 1905. (G. Burton)

A view from the top of Brook Street looking up Wells Walk and Wells Promenade, February 1933. (Bradford Galleries and Museums)

'Tobogganing at Ilkley', January 1909. Young folk pose for the camera in Wells Road. The Royal Hotel is on the left. (M. Dixon)

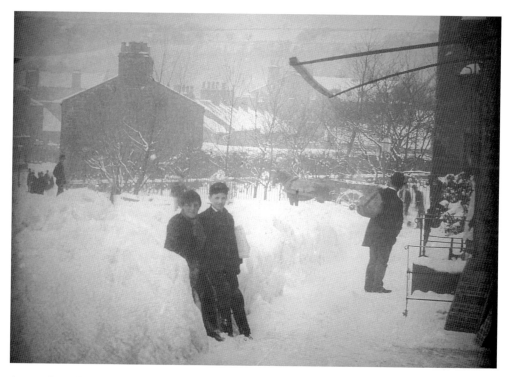

A view from the foot of Wells Road after a heavy snow fall, 1902. (M. Dixon)

Wells Road in the snow, February 1933. The railings on the left belong to Wells Road Methodist Church and were removed, like many others, during the Second World War. The church was demolished in 1970 to be replaced by Guardian Court. (Bradford Galleries and Museums)

Snow in South Hawksworth Street, *c.* 1910. The low buildings on the right (now demolished) were the stables behind the Rose and Crown Hotel. Cunliffe Road crosses from left to right at the foot of the street. The area to the left, now the central car park, was occupied by a nursery (market garden) and allotments, while across Cunliffe Road was the bowling green behind the Lister's Arms Hotel. The railway viaduct dominates the background. (G. Burton)

Above: Council workers using a horse-drawn plough to clear snow outside the Royal Hotel in the 1940s. At that time the Council had several working horses under the charge of Mr Billy Woodrup. The horses were stabled in Golden Butts Road but were put out to graze on land beside the swimming pool, later the Olicanians cricket ground. (M. Dixon)

Right: Snow Patrol – December 1981. Two policemen cope with the snow near Leconfield House. Leconfield was opened in 1974 on land previously occupied by Tower Buildings. The latter was the subject of compulsory purchase by the Council who intended to provide a roundabout with offices and a petrol station. This scheme did not materialise and instead sheltered housing and, later a mini-roundabout, were constructed. (B. Marshall/*Ilkley Gazette*)

Skating on the Tarn, 25 December 1960. Sunshine and keen frost provided excellent conditions for skating on Christmas Day morning. The skating conditions were further enhanced by the actions of the Fire Brigade. At the Council's behest, they would bring a pump up to the Tarn each evening, break a hole in the ice, insert a hose and pump water to spray over the surface of the ice to renew it for the next day's skating. Now all we get are warnings about the dangers of skating on thin ice. (*Ilkley Gazette*)

An ice wheel (Crum wheel) on River Wharfe, January 1907. Very occasionally during a deep frost, the wheel forms in the whirlpool found at this bend in the river. The origin of the name 'Crum' is obscure but could be derived from the Old English pre-seventh-century word 'crumb' (or 'crump') meaning bent or crooked. (M. Dixon)

4

WORKERS AND PLAYERS

Ilkley postmen, 1905. The post office was situated in Wells Road and the office staff, including the postmaster, Mr R.A. Moffat (fourth from the left), join the postmen, telegraph boys and a dog, in this group photograph. The shop on the right belongs to John Rhodes, tinner and ironmonger, while above the post office is C.A. Broadhead, jeweller and silversmith, maker of the renowned 'Ilkley Souvenir Spoon'. Above this double-fronted shop is the caretaker's house adjoining the Wesleyan Church, a site now occupied by Guardian Court. (W. Porritt)

Mr William Bradley – local inventor, 1937. Bill was born in Ilkley in 1885 and trained in engineering before emigrating to Canada. He returned in 1908 because he didn't fancy his prospects there, and he opened a garage in Addingham. Bill was a motorcycle pioneer and many of his inventions related to engines and gearboxes, but he also turned his hand to textile machines. The scale-model shown here won him the Hoffman Wood Gold Medal for the best non-war invention of the year. Unfortunately, we are not told what the machine does! (M. Cawood)

Men attending the Ilkley Unemployed Centre take part in an outdoor Physical Education class, 1932. The centre was situated in Marshfield, a house next to the post office in Leeds Road. It closed in 1933 due to a lack of enthusiasm on the part of the unemployed. Although there were almost 200 men out of work in Ilkley in February 1933, there had been only five or six attending the centre each day. (*Ilkley Gazette*)

Above: Ilkley Sheep Dog Trials, 1937. During the 1930s the trials were held annually in Denton Park by courtesy of Mr and Mrs Arthur Hill of Denton Hall. The three judges (on the left) are Messrs J. Ackrigg, F.S. White and T. Pighills, and others in the picture are Messrs C. Saville (time-keeper), H.S. Redshaw (Hon. Secretary), C. Hardisty and A. Hayton, together with some of the competitors, both human and canine. (M. Cawood)

Right: Shepherd's rest. Mark Hayton, of Ilkley, and his son Arthur (nearest the camera) watch the Sheep Dog Trials at Denton Park in 1938. Arthur Hayton won the Shepherds' Class for the fifth year in succession. (M. Cawood)

Breakfast's on the dot nowadays

thanks to PUBLIC SERVANT NO. 1

The oven-heat on a gas cooker is automatically controlled— put a whole dinner in the oven, leave it, and come back to find it perfectly cooked.

GAS

PUBLIC SERVANT No. 1

never lets you down — gives you more time off!

Ilkley Urban District Council Gas Dept.

LEEDS ROAD, ILKLEY.

Telephone No. 95.

Left: 'Gas – Public Servant No. 1'; an advertisement of 1937 that underlines the stereotype of women's 'work'. 'Gas – never lets you down, gives you more time off'; 'Put a whole dinner in the oven, leave it, and come back to find it perfectly cooked.' Unlikely. (M. Dixon)

Below: Making hay, West Moor House farm, Middleton, *c.* 1940. A worker lifts a bundle of hay with either a rake or a pitchfork onto the cart while the farmer, Mr Rigg, clears up the last of a field-cock or 'hub', leaving behind the three-legged supporting frame that aids drying. An intact field-cock, a pile of hay about 7-8ft high, can be seen behind. (C.M. Duncan)

Above: Loading oats for the stack-yard on Mr Tidyman's farm, Home Farm, Denton, *c.* 1940. (C.M. Duncan)

Right: Tea-break, *c.* 1940. A building worker takes his turn to make the tea. The enamel mugs and the brazier to heat the kettle are now largely things of the past. (C.M. Duncan)

Potato digging, *c.* 1942. In keeping with the war-time movement towards self-sufficiency in food production – 'Dig for Victory' – the National School's playing field on Leeds Road (now Ashlands School site) was given over to potato growing. Here, the team get ready for lifting the 'spuds'. Ted Hinchcliffe, a local butcher, looks after the horse. In the background are houses on Dean Street and the line of trees marks the edge of Leeds Road. (C.M. Duncan)

The young potato pickers (assisted by some older folk) scrabble around in the soil. (C.M. Duncan)

Harvest time on East Holmes field, 1946. The field adjacent to the rugby ground (Stack's Field) had been given over to cereal growing for the first time since the First World War. The field yielded between eight and ten tons of oats, which were used to feed horses owned by the Urban District Council. (C.M. Duncan)

A 'Victory' party held at the end of the Second World War in 1945. The party was for children living in the vicinity of Leeds Road and was held in the Primitive Methodist church hall. The elderly lady is poised to cut the 'Victory' cake but it doesn't look as if it will go far among the throng of hungry children. Its small size no doubt reflects war-time rationing! (Win Porritt)

Sam Rayner, the last of six generations of blacksmiths in Ilkley, announces his retirement, May 1959. The blacksmith's shop was off Little Lane behind the Co-op (more recently Cooper's Antiques) but by 1959 there just weren't enough horses to shoe, or cart-wheels to hoop, to sustain the business. (A. Anning/*Ilkley Gazette*)

An electric carpet cleaner at Porritt's, Railway Road, 1995. John Porritt is feeding a stair carpet into an electric carpet-beating machine purchased by his grandfather in 1920 at an exhibition in Port Sunlight organised by a Mr Lever, a man who went on to do big things! It was the first such machine in the area and enabled Porritt's to 'corner the market' in carpet cleaning. Given the number of large houses in Ilkley there would be no shortage of work. John had taken over the business in 1966 on the death of his father, Fred Porritt. (Win Porritt)

Building work outside the Leeds Road Congregational Hall, 1961. The Hall closed in May 1970 and was demolished soon after. (N.R. Thompson/*Ilkley Gazette*)

'The Coronets' at the Pavilion, Riverside Gardens, 1910, another seasonal theatrical offering to compete with the celebrated Tarn Pierrots. (T. Mutton)

A home for the Players, *c*. 1960. The building in the background was shared between the Liberal Club, on the ground floor, and the Ilkley Players who rented the room upstairs. Most of the time the relationship was harmonious, though on occasions a tense moment on stage would be shattered by a roar from below when someone hit a 'double top' to win the darts match. The Liberals had a large number of young male members at that time because the club had the best snooker tables in Ilkley. Ladies could not be members of the club. (A. Anning/*Ilkley Gazette*)

Ilkley Players perform *Busman's Holiday*, October 1938. Originally a book by Dorothy L. Sayers in the Lord Peter Wimsey series, it was adapted for the stage and first performed in December 1936. The players are, from left to right: Harold Cockcroft (a stalwart at the Playhouse), Basil Rookes, Basil Smith, Ronald Priestman and John Ingram. (A. Anning/*Ilkley Gazette*)

Music players – Bradley Hustwick's band play at the Craiglands Hotel, 1954. The line-up was, from left to right: Reggie Dove (piano), Bill Smith (compère), Bob Hopkinson (violin), Harry Roe (drums) and Bradley Hustwick and Dennis Petty (accordions). Bradley's band also provided the music for the Saturday night dances in the Essoldo cinema ballroom. Mr Hopkinson became stone deaf in later years so the drummer would tap out the rhythm of the tune on Bob's shoulder until he was into his stride. (F.W. Smith)

The circus comes to town, 1957. Crowds lined Brook Street to watch this parade of camels and elephants from Chipperfield's Circus, which was paying its first visit to Ilkley. The animals arrived by train and were unloaded at the cattle dock in the goods sidings alongside Station Road. The animals were then led in procession to their quarters near the Big Top on the Grammar School playing field in Ben Rhydding. The manager of the circus apologised for not holding a full parade with their vehicles because of petrol rationing. (M. Dixon)

More Ilkley thespians, 1937. Members of the Ilkley Amateur Operatic Company perform *The Student Prince* at the King's Hall. The somewhat 'mature students' were Leslie Watson (as Hubert), Harold Cockroft (Lutz), Kay Smith (Gretchen), Jessie Dawtrey (Kathie) and Will Owen (Ruder). (M. Dixon)

Music Hall comes to Ilkley, 1963. Ilkley Round Table held this parade of old vehicles to publicise their Old Tyme Music Hall. The wagonette at the front used to ply between Ilkley and Bolton Abbey. Alf Simpson (holding the reins) found it under a pile of hay at Emmanuel Pratt's farm in Draughton and it was refurbished by Table members with help from Chambers Brothers' vehicle paint-shop in Castle Road. The car behind is a 1906 Renault that belonged to Dr Marshman, a GP in Keighley. One of his patients was Mr Peter Black, and Marshman sold him a 1922 Rolls-Royce Silver Ghost, the first in what was to become a remarkable collection of vintage cars. (D.R. Powell/ *Ilkley Gazette*)

5

CRICKET AND CARNIVAL

The third Black Hats versus White Hats Cricket Match, September 1882. In 1879 a member of Ilkley Cricket Club, then facing serious financial difficulties, hit on the idea of a fund-raising novelty cricket match to coincide with the Ilkley Feast. The first match took place in 1880 when two teams made up of local tradesmen, each with about twenty players, took to the field – then situated off Railway Road. 1882 was the first year that the players distinguished themselves by donning black or white hats and thereafter these became *de rigeur*. The Black Hats were captained by John Beanlands and the White Hats by the veteran, William Lister. (M. Dixon)

The teams in 1889. This year saw a switch to playing the match on a Wednesday afternoon as it was half-day closing for the shops. That practice was followed thereafter. Mr John Beanlands captained the 'White Hat Brigade' while Mr James Critchley captained the opposition. 'Combatants who were known to be above average as trundlers of the leather, or wielders of the willow, were handicapped in various ways; for instance, the wearers of hats with a single x upon them were not allowed to bowl at all; while those marked xx, were not allowed to bowl and were obliged to bat left-handedly.' (M. Dixon)

The players in the Black Hats versus White Hats cricket match of September 1896. In 1892 a handsome silver cup was purchased by subscription among the tradesmen and offered for annual competition. The trophy is held by a distinguished-looking gentleman bearing a striking resemblance to the Prince of Wales and who wears a white hat with a black band, presumably a neutral non-combatant! (M. Dixon)

The Black and White Hats 'coming of age',
1901. The twenty-first annual match was
celebrated with a dinner at Lister's Arms
Hotel. The former captains had by now
risen to the rank of elder statesmen, Messrs
Beanlands and Lister occupying the offices
of Chairman and Vice-Chairman. The
menu would have given no comfort to a
vegetarian – oxtail soup followed by cod fish
and oyster sauce, jugged hare, roast beef,
boiled leg of mutton, roast veal and York
ham. For dessert there were Edward VII and
Coming-of-Age puddings and, just to fill any
empty crevices, cheese and celery to finish.
(M. Dixon)

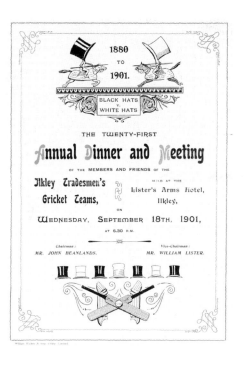

Ilkley Carnival Procession, 1909. By 1885 the novelty cricket match was firmly established
in the Ilkley calendar and in that year it was decided to capitalise on the fun and frivolity
surrounding the event by holding a carnival procession. The procession would assemble
outside the Town Hall and proceed around the town via The Grove, Bolton Bridge Road,
Skipton Road, Church Street and Brook Street to end at the cricket ground and join the
antics of the players. Here, the soldier on horseback leads the procession, headed by morris
dancers and the town band, from Bolton Bridge Road into Skipton Road. (M. Dixon)

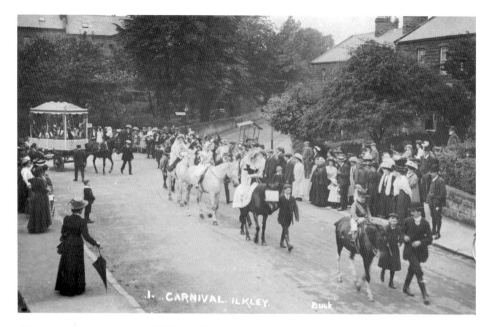

Ilkley Carnival Procession, 1909. A little later and the crowd had increased to watch the fancy-dress horse riders and the decorated drays. (M. Dixon)

Ilkley Carnival, August Bank Holiday, 1911. The carnival was now a separate event held a month before the cricket match. The procession assembles in glorious weather outside the Town Hall under the supervision of the marshall, Mr J. Weatherill (in the boater) and another member of the committee (in the trilby hat). The president of the carnival that year was the Revd F. Sinker, vicar of All Saints. The procession started off at 1.30 p.m. and made its way to the Holmes, where the fancy-dress costumes were judged and the prizes awarded. In addition there were displays by a detachment of the Yorkshire Hussars, athletic competitions, stalls and side-shows. (Bradford Galleries and Museums)

Ilkley Carnival Procession before the First World War makes its way down Brook Street. The shops on the east side of the street reflect the differing shopping needs of the day and comprise the Wharncliffe Restaurant and Coffee Tavern, Maud Gains (milliner), John Thwaites (tobacconist and hairdresser), Walter Cook (harness maker), and Henry Hudson (bootmaker). (Bradford Galleries and Museums)

The Black Hats versus White Hats teams of 1920. In this match there were thirty-seven men in each team. Admission to the ground cost 5d. (M. Dixon)

The carnival: three generations of Porritts take part in the fancy-dress parade, *c.* 1930. On the left is Sam (Councillor John Samuel Porritt), while granddaughter Jean is in the arms of Sam's son, Fred. Sam founded an upholstery business in Railway Road in the 1920s with Fred also working in the business (J.S. Porritt & Son). As a town councillor, Sam was largely instrumental in getting the paddling pool constructed on the edge of Ilkley Moor. Hence, for some years after it was affectionately known by the locals as 'Porritt's Pool'. (M. Dixon)

Ilkley Carnival ladies fancy-dress competition, 1934. (M. Dixon)

A carnival scene (undated). One of the fancy-dress contestants is attempting to appeal to the judges with a placard proclaiming 'Ilkley – glory of Moor and Dale'. The gentleman in the top hat fails to see anything amusing in the whole business. (M. Dixon)

A carnival 'float' in Railway Road, *c.* 1935. The lorry, a Morris Commercial, belonged to J.S. Porritt & Son. The sign in the background indicates George Mennell's yard. Originally in a partnership as 'Mennell and Dean – Coal and Coke Merchants', Mr Dean died and Mr Mennell carried on the business, later branching out into house removals. George Mennell also served as honorary superintendent of the volunteer fire brigade. The site of Mennell's yard is now occupied by four semi-detached houses. (Win Porritt)

A group pose prior to the cricket match in 1932. Although there are numerous ladies in the photograph, and several are wearing white top-hats, this is pure frivolity. At this stage ladies were not permitted to play in the Tradesmen's event. (M. Dixon)

A pre-match publicity photograph, 1934 – a significant year as it was the first match in which ladies were allowed to play. Although a lady holds the trophy, she was not one of the captains. The fairer sex only rose to captaincy in 1937 when Miss P. Wellen, whose mother had a confectionary shop in Brook Street, captained the White Hats. The Black Hats won. The matches were discontinued after the outbreak of the Second World War. There was a short-lived revival after the war with matches from 1945 to 1948, but post-war austerity did not seem suited to zany cricket matches and they fell into abeyance. (M. Dixon)

The Tradesmen's Winners and Loser's Cups are discovered in the attic of the Manor House Museum by the Curator, Steve Kerry (with the moustache), and museum staff, *c.* 1977. The trophies had been 'lost' for several years. Apparently they were placed in the museum for safe keeping in anticipation of local government reorganisation, but the original depositor didn't tell anyone. The finding of the Cups inspired local photographer Richard Beckwith and other members of the Chamber of Trade to revive the matches. The new lease of life began with a match on Sunday, 24 September 1978, under the captainship of Denis Coplestone (Black Hats) and Dick Beckwith (White Hats). (R. Beckwith/M. Dixon)

The Centenary Celebration Match, May Bank Holiday 1980. Andrew Sharpe, captain of the White Hats, shares a joke with Judith Chalmers and holds the victor's cup. The White Hats scored 147 for 19 wickets while the Black Hats could only muster 117 runs for 18 wickets. The White Hats, however, held a significant advantage in having three former Yorkshire and England cricketers in the team – Don Wilson, Brian Close and Freddie Trueman; little wonder that they beat their less accomplished opponents. Before the Centenary Match, the event commenced with a procession of decorated floats through the town – prompting the idea that the carnival should also be revived. (M. Dixon)

The Centenary Celebration Match 1980. Freddie Trueman draws a ticket from the Prize Draw box under the watchful eyes of organiser Dennis Read and the then landlord of the Fleece Hotel, Addingham, David Harrison. Earlier in the afternoon Freddie had caused consternation by slogging a 'six' into the crowd and the ball knocked out an elderly lady spectator. Fortunately she soon recovered consciousness (under observation by a neurosurgeon, who just happened to be present). After a check-up at hospital, she was able to go home the same day. (M. Dixon)

The Centenary Celebration Match 1980. The Lord Mayor of Bradford, Councillor John Senior, presents the Loser's Trophy to the captain of the Black Hats, Walter Forrest. (M. Dixon)

6

SERVING THE COMMUNITY

1st Lancashire Royal Engineer Volunteers march up Bolton Bridge Road, close to the junction with The Grove, 1905. The parade is headed by the Cyclists Section, followed by the band and then the infantry soldiers. They were probably taking the long route from their camp on the East Holmes field to the railway station, where they embarked for the return to Lancashire. (T. Mutton)

'D' Company, Yorkshire Bantams, marching up New Brook Street. In 1914 the Member of Parliament for Birkenhead, Alfred Bigland, pressed the War Office for permission to form a battalion of men who were under regulation height (5ft 3in) but otherwise fit for service. A few days later, some 3,000 men had volunteered in Birkenhead, many of whom had previously been rejected as being under height. Several regiments, including the West Yorkshire Regiment (Prince of Wales' Own), went on to raise Bantam Battalions. The 17th West Yorkshire Bantams were raised in December 1914 and during part of 1915 were billeted in Ilkley. In June 1915, a Bantam's officer, Ernest Roscoe, was fatally injured while travelling with other officers in a car from Ilkley to Skipton. (T. Mutton)

'Kitchen Staff Ben Rhydding' (Hydro), First World War period. The two soldiers in the group are members of the West Yorkshire Regiment. The soldier at the front with the tipsy hat may be saying his farewells to the young kitchen maid, while (judging from her expression) the older lady behind will make sure that events do not turn too amorous! (M. Dixon)

Above: The Town Hall, library and King's Hall, *c.* 1951. These buildings have been serving the community since their opening on 27 April 1908. The first council meeting in the new chamber was held on 6 May 1908. The Winter Gardens on the right were added later and opened in 1913. (A. Anning/M. Dixon)

Right: Egg collection for 'The Voluntary Hospitals of the West Riding' outside Mr Dalton's shop at the corner of The Grove and Brook Street, 1937. One of the more unusual ways of helping hospital expenses was the holding of the annual 'Egg Day', when people contributed eggs which were then stored and used to supplement the patients' diet for months afterwards. This particular 'Mr Dalton' was Billy, brother of Percy and Jim, a big man who played in the forwards at Ilkley Rugby Club. (C.M. Duncan).

Ilkley Firemen aboard their 'new' engine in the Golden Butts station yard, *c.* 1940. The engine had been commissioned in October 1939, but not without some criticism from the rate-payers who considered the old engine to be entirely adequate. Replying to the comments, Councillor A.C. Voigt explained that 'The old machine was doing its work very efficiently but it was not able, like some old people, to get up some of the lovely Ilkley hills as quickly as necessary in case of fire.' The new engine, an eight-cylinder Leyland FK, was capable of pumping 700 gallons of water a minute to a height greater than any building in Ilkley. One of the headlights is equipped with a war-time blackout shield. (C.M. Duncan).

Red Cross volunteer nurses (and male orderlies), *c.* 1943. The group are photographed outside the 'Sick Bay', a converted house at the corner of Alexander Crescent and Lister Street, where cadets and officers belonging to the Ilkley-based OTC would be cared for during illness. Seated at the centre of the front row is Mrs J.C. Ford of The Pines, Parish Ghyll Drive. She was a leading light in the Red Cross – and in Ilkley society. Her husband was a director of the now defunct Melbourne Brewery of Plum Street, Leeds. Her daughter, seated immediately to her right, married an officer called Pye-Smith during the war. He died shortly after the war and she subsequently married an Ilkley GP, Dr Plummer, and moved into Carlton House in The Grove. (D. Craven)

A visit from Princess Mary to S.U. Carburettors at Low Mill. In 1941 the S.U. Carburettors factory in Coventry was bombed, and production was moved to Low Mill, a former textile factory. Up to 1,000 people worked there and a large number of prefabricated houses had to be erected in Ilkley to house them. The 'prefabs', built on vacant land to the west of Victoria Avenue, were 'temporary' wartime structures that served as council housing until their demolition in 1966. During the war, Princess Mary, daughter of King George V and wife of the Earl of Harewood, travelled Britain visiting women's territorial units, wartime canteens and other welfare organisations. (D. Craven)

On the occasion of Princess Mary's visit, those members of staff who had volunteered for First Aid duties, including Red Cross volunteers, showed off their marching skills. (D. Craven)

Air Training Corps No. 1224 Ilkley Squadron, August 1942. The cadets are assembled under the nose of a gargantuan Lancaster bomber on an airfield visit. The Lancasters were made at the A.V. Roe (AVRO) factory in Yeadon where around 700 of these bombers were produced during the Second World War. (M. Dixon)

The 1st Ilkley (All Saints' Church) Wolf Cubs, Brownies, Guides and Scouts, c. 1932. The group have assembled outside Skelda Grange, in Wells Road, formerly the vicarage of the parish church. The group leader at this time was Mr Arthur E. Pickett (first man from left, seated on second row). He was a man of considerable scouting experience and enthusiasm. He even conducted a troop choir that entered the Wharfedale Festival. After the performance, the adjudicator (Julius Harrison) commented on the choir's rhythm and tone and awarded them a respectable eighty-one points. Hearing the score, the troop responded with the cry, 'Mr Julius Harrison, Hurrah, Hurrah, Hurrah.' As he was heading back to his seat, Mr Harrison immediately turned around and declared, 'fifty for rhythm, none for tone.' (D. Craven)

A scout parade marches from Church Street into Brook Street, 1930s. The pub on the corner, the Wheatsheaf, is one of Ilkley's oldest hostelries. The Wheatsheaf was derived from the crest of the Middelton family. The pub was demolished in 1959 and the site given over to the gardens around All Saints' Church. (A. Walbank)

Ilkley Guides parade on Empire Day into St Margaret's Church, *c.* 1935. There were several guide companies in the town; pictured here are members of the 6th Ilkley Guides about to enter the church. Empire Day was instituted in 1904 and was held on 24 May, the birthday of Queen Victoria. It was a day redolent with patriotic fervour. At these church parades the vicar would regale the assembled throng on the subject of God, King and Country, and the great British Empire, combined with such uplifting songs as 'Jerusalem' and 'Land of Hope and Glory'. (*Ilkley Gazette*)

Guides in camp at Robin Hole, Burley Woodhead, Easter 1958. The redoubtable Miss Phyllis Holmes of Addingham, a prominent guider in the district, stands in the middle of the second from back row, flanked by Ann Shepherd and Mary Wetherall. (A. Anning/*Ilkley Gazette*)

Scouts march up Church Street in a St George's Day parade, 1964. The parade is lead by Flag-Bearer David Wilde, and, from left to right: Phillip Conyers (Scout Commissioner), Fred Sweet (Scout Leader) and Eric 'Gunner' Maufe (District Commissioner). Colonel Maufe was a member of the Muff/Maufe family of Brown Muff store fame in Bradford. He served with distinction in the First World War gaining the MC and bar. (N.R. Thompson/*Ilkley Gazette*)

Ilkley Hospital, *c.* 1905. The hospital was opened in 1862 under the auspices of the Ilkley Bath Charitable Institution which had been founded in 1829 by the curate George Fenton. The institution provided bath treatment for the poor. Subscribers paid 21*s* per year and this enabled them to nominate a person for a three-week stay at the hospital. The building, with a capacity of seventy beds, cost only £3,016 including fittings. In 1885 the hospital was enlarged at a cost of £2,960 so that up to 100 patients could be accommodated. The hospital closed in 1993 and after being unoccupied for several years, it was purchased and developed by the Ilkley Abbeyfield Society. It re-opened in 2004 as 'Grove House'. (M. Dixon)

The putting green, Ilkley Hospital and Convalescent Home in the 1930s – a ladies' competition is in progress. (M. Dixon)

Semon Convalescent Home, 1950s. Charles Semon was a wealthy Bradford merchant who in 1874 built the Convalescent Home that carried his name at a cost of £12,000. In 1876 Semon presented the Home together with an endowment of £3,000 to Bradford Corporation. The Home was 'to be used exclusively for persons of slender means whether born in the United Kingdom or elsewhere, and whether resident in Bradford or not, who are in a weak state of health, or who, having been ill, are tardily recovering and require for complete restoration to health good food, rest and kind treatment together with medical supervision'. The Home was demolished in 1995 and replaced by the Westwood Rise housing development. (T. Mutton)

The dining room at Semon Convalescent Home, 1930s. 'The Home and surroundings are splendid,' writes the sender of the postcard. 'There are between 90 and 100 in the Home. All like one big family and so jolly. We are having a concert tonight.' (M. Dixon)

Ardenlea, North Eastern Railwaymen's Convalescent Home, 1930s. A letter from Simeon Hardwick, a goods guard from Darlington, relates, 'I cannot express the deep gratitude I feel for the treatment I received during the fourteen days I have spent at Ardenlea, Ilkley. I went into that institution on 11 August and am now at my home completely recovered. I earnestly commend the Home to NE [North Eastern] men, and hope that they will take advantage of the opportunity to subscribe (half penny per week) to the home away from home, where every facility is given to regain lost health. I enclose a small donation of 10s, my only regret being that I cannot afford £10.' (M. Dixon)

A group of men assemble outside the Railwaymen's Convalescent Home along with the matron and her dog, c. 1925. The two men on either side of the matron wear arm-bands bearing a sergeant's and corporal's stripes; they would have been chosen as organisers of 'volunteer' duties and social events in the Home and given 'honorary officer' status. The Home closed in 1963 and was purchased by the Marie Curie Foundation. The building was sold and converted into apartments in 2003. (M. Dixon)

Left: Mrs Clara Hayward standing outside the former Isolation Hospital, *c.* 1930. The building, opened by the Local Board as a cottage hospital in April 1888, was situated near the river. Constructed of corrugated iron on a wooden frame, the hospital had two four-bed wards separated by a room used for 'administration'. Its function as a cottage hospital, where patients were treated by their own medical attendants, was taken over by the Coronation Hospital in 1905. Thereafter it was used as the Isolation ('Fever') Hospital. Its position, wedged between the sewage works and the cemetery, was certainly conducive to isolation. Sometime after 1910, the hospital was converted into a house and was let to Mr Hayward, who was employed at the Sewage Works. (Joan Williams)

Below: A gathering of staff marks the retirement of Matron Langdon from the Coronation Hospital in 1953. The Matron is seated fourth from the left in the middle row. Local GPs, Drs Gott, Whamond, Plummer, Ferris, Armstrong and Frost, are present, as well as Sisters Brailsford, Browning and Thornton and other nurses, the secretaries and ancillary staff. (A. Anning/M. Dixon)

7

BROOK STREET AND
THE GROVE

A view of the top of Brook Street, *c.* 1870. The original Station Hotel (landlord William Dobson) is on the left, while just beyond is the diminutive cruck-built grocery shop of Joseph Ickringill. At the foot of Brook Street stands the Wheatsheaf Hotel (left) and the original Star Inn stand at the entrance to Leeds Road. (Bradford Galleries and Museums)

The east side of Brook Street, *c.* 1875. The conversion of houses into shops on this side of the street is not yet complete. A sign indicates access to the stables in the Crescent yard, while there is ample evidence of previous horse-drawn traffic on the road outside. (Bradford Galleries and Museums)

Demolition work in Brook Street, 1885. Once the Midland Railway had received Parliamentary approval for the extension of the line from Ilkley to Skipton, their contractors set about preparing the way for the bridge across Brook Street. Work commenced in June 1885. The thatched cottage had belonged to William Shoesmith, a greengrocer. The next-door shop of Richardson, the boot-maker, and the original Station Hotel were also demolished. (G. Burton)

Right: Earnshaw's, Brook Street, *c.* 1901. Mr A. Earnshaw was Ilkley's foremost clockmaker, jeweller and silversmith. His lasting claim to fame was that he made the enamelled medallions that were presented to dignitaries after they had performed some public ceremony. So, for example, Earnshaw made two splendid ceremonial keys for the Revd Robert Collyer and Andrew Carnegie to mark the opening of the library in 1907. (M. Dixon)

Below: A view of the bottom of Brook Street showing the new Star Inn, 1905. The building of the new bridge and laying down of New Brook Street necessitated the demolition of a number of buildings around the bottom of Brook Street, including the original Star Inn, the Wharfedale Inn next door and the old gas works behind. The opportunity was taken to set the new Star Inn further back to remove the former dog-leg bend from Church Street into Leeds Road. Nothing was done, however, about the lamp post and the postbox, which remained as traffic hazards for years to come. (M. Dixon)

Brook Street, *c.* 1911. On the left, the lamp post and postbox still stand defiantly in the middle of the road. The lamp post may have been retained in this position because it doubled as a ventilator for the culvert (carrying the brook under Brook Street) – the post is unusually substantial and there is an open vent immediately beneath the lamp housing. (T. Mutton)

The top of Brook Street, *c.* 1912. Looking under the bridge, the continuation of the road as New Brook Street can be clearly seen. The building lines at the sides of Brook Street were established when there was both a carriageway and a brook running down it. This explains its unusual width, how Ilkley's cab stand could be accommodated down the middle of the street. (M. Dixon)

The top of Brook Street, *c.* 1934. The street is dominated by the railway bridge, an ugly structure but providing the unexpected benefit of a covered meeting place. Many dates were made with the arrangement, 'I'll meet you under the bridge.' Behind the bus is Lionel Bubb's newsagent's shop, while next door Mrs Annie Wilkinson presided over her fruit and flower shop. She had a second shop in the station approach. (F.W. Smith)

The top of Brook Street in 1957. On the right is yet another materialisation of Peggy's Café, separated by the snicket that led up to the station forecourt from Greenwood's gentlemen's outfitters. Lower down is Woolworth's with its once characteristic and universal (maroon) fascia – F.W. Woolworth & Co. Ltd. (T. Mutton)

The fountain at the top of Brook Street, *c.* 1950. The fountain was erected in 1875 at a cost of £130, paid for by public subscription. The original was an ornate affair with mermaids and four large horses whose nostrils spouted water. A further twenty-one jets sprayed water into the bowl of the fountain. Water was fed by gravity from a supply tank at the top of Mill Ghyll located just below the Royal Hotel. Following damage to the original fountain, it was replaced by this simpler pile of rocks, but even this rudimentary structure was subjected to further vandalism and was removed in 1959. G. Burton)

A resting place at the top of Brook Street, *c.* 1960. Dalton's was a butcher's shop; next door was Boots the chemists. Busby's was a 'superior' ladies' fashion shop – a branch of the famous department store in Manningham Lane, Bradford. Next came the Yorkshire Penny Bank, and finally Barclay's Bank, occupying a distinguished building erected for the Bradford Old Bank. Billy Dalton was a well-known, and irascible, Ilkley character. He would attend Skipton Auction Mart on Friday mornings to buy animals for slaughter, and would enjoy a long liquid lunch before returning to his shop. This did nothing for his temper, and Friday afternoon was certainly not the time to enter his shop if you hadn't paid your bill! (M. Dixon)

More shops in Brook Street, 1950s. At the bottom of the street was Dormand Stewarts, a shop specialising in waterproof coats. Their slogan, written across the bottom of the window, was 'We shall have rain' – a self-evident truth in Ilkley! Next door was Redman's, the grocer's; then Robinson's, a gentlemen's outfitters; followed by Fred Tree's greengrocery and fish shop. Next was Mott's china shop (where Boots is now); Burrell's cheese shop; Clayton's, pork butchers; Scott's the chemists; and on the corner of West Street, Hardingham's confectionary shop. On the opposite corner was Lloyd's Bank (as now); then Melias, grocers; Wilfred Denton, tailor and outfitter; William Lawson, plumber; Hills, jewellers and Dewhurst's, butchers. (M. Dixon)

Brook Street bridge demolition, 1966. Once the line closed in 1965, contractors were appointed to lift the rails and remove the bridge. On Sunday, 10 July 1966, the street was closed at 5 a.m. and a large mobile crane lifted down the two spans into the road. Engineers cut the spans into two, and the four sections were taken to the old goods siding for further dismantling. A few days later the western abutment was removed, thereby clearing a pedestrian way into the central car park. In a matter of days, Brook Street had been transformed. (P.A. Thornton)

Left: Burrell's cheese shop, Brook Street, 1991. Before opening his own shop in Ilkley, Mr Burrell had been manager of Carr's Grocers in Burley-in-Wharfedale. Mr Burrell behaved like a well-known Dickens character – 'very 'umble' – and lady customers were invariably greeted by a hand-rubbing Mr Burrell asking, 'Can I help you, Madam?' He was not so solicitous with the men.
(A.M. Grunwell)

Below: The Grove, 1905. It is not widely appreciated that The Grove starts at the corner of Wells Road. The two shops on the extreme left belonged to Alfred Vickers who sold 'fancy goods' (and whose main shop was in Leeds) and C.E. Knight, a stationer. Some time before 1912 these shops, numbered 3 and 5 The Grove, were acquired by the London City and Midland Bank Ltd and converted into their Ilkley branch.
(M. Dixon)

The Grove in the 1930s. The bank has by now vacated its corner site in favour of Peggy's Café but the stone facing and mullioned windows continue to lend distinction to the property. The heraldic shield of the bank can still be seen in the wall on the Wells Promenade aspect of the building. Peggy's Café was an Ilkley institution for many years, although it tended to move around! After occupying this corner, it displaced Eva Kitson from her confectionary shop and occupied the corner of Wells Road for some years. Thereafter it had a brief sojourn across the road on the corner of Brook Street before disappearing from the Ilkley scene. The seats comprising the 'monkey-rack' are well filled. (G. Burton)

The Grove, c. 1922. A different perspective shows the fountain and its encircling ring of chattering sitters, the horse trough, and two splendid cars – a 'bull-nose' Morris on the right and a Calthorpe two-seater alongside. On the corner is the Craven Bank while next door is William Rhodes' china and glass shop. Edward Hargreaves was a hairdresser and an importer of high-class cigars. Literally thousands of fine Havanas were stored in a specially constructed room where they were gradually 'conditioned' prior to sale. (T. Mutton)

The Grove looking east, *c.* 1904. Note the Ilkley branch of the York City and County Banking Co. Ltd (second on the left). In 1905 the bank moved to newly built and much enlarged premises at the corner of Wells Road (now HSBC). (T. Mutton)

The Grove, *c.* 1910. The ladies' fashions emphasise that The Grove has always been a place to promenade as well as shop. On the left, an elderly woman is helped into her bath chair. Next to the Misses Annie and Lilian Brownhill's Art and Needlework Repository is the shop of Messrs Johnson Brothers, Dyers and Cleaners, while the next-door premises are of particular interest. The shop on the ground floor (at No. 40) belonged to Taylor's Drug Co. while above it, and indicated by a 'bell' sign, was the Public Call Office of the National Telephone Co. Ltd – Ilkley's first telephone exchange. (M. Dixon)

Above: Café Imperial and Ellis Beanlands' shop in The Grove, 1964. The Café Imperial occupies a building erected in 1884 for William Scott, the photographer. The Imperial and another café in The Grove, the Kiosk, were owned by C.E. Taylor & Co., the Harrogate tea merchants. Following the takeover of Taylor's by Betty's in 1962, Taylor's cafés were gradually closed down. Betty's chose to develop the Kiosk café site for their tea-rooms in Ilkley. Ellis Beanlands' was one of four grocery shops in the town owned by the Beanlands brothers; the others being in the Arcade, in Brook Street, and Ben Rhydding. Their shops did not survive the challenge of the supermarkets. (P.A. Thornton)

Right: An advertisement for Dinsdale & Co., The Grove, 1927. Dinsdales took over two adjacent shops in 1898 and converted them into a wine, spirit and tobacco emporium. They installed mosaics in the doorways displaying the monogram 'D&Co' which are still there today, as is the carving of a bunch of grapes on the door of the Cancer Research shop! No doubt their Swastika Whisky fell out of favour during the 1930s, despite the symbol's valid historical connection with the town. (M. Dixon)

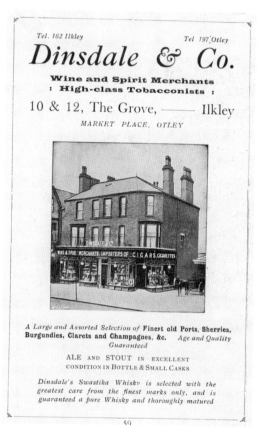

Tel. 162 Ilkley   Tel 197 Otley

Dinsdale & Co.

Wine and Spirit Merchants
: High-class Tobacconists :

10 & 12, The Grove, —— Ilkley

MARKET PLACE, OTLEY

A Large and Assorted Selection of **Finest old Ports, Sherries, Burgundies, Clarets and Champagnes, &c.** *Age and Quality Guaranteed*

ALE AND STOUT IN EXCELLENT CONDITION IN BOTTLE & SMALL CASKS

Dinsdale's Swastika Whisky is selected with the greatest care from the finest marks only, and is guaranteed a pure Whisky and thoroughly matured

59

The Grove, *c.* 1947. The building on the right is The Spa, a former hydropathic hotel converted into apartments and a café in 1919. Initially the café was also called The Spa, but by this time it is known as the Blue Bird café. (T. Mutton)

The 'Canker Well' Gardens looking towards Cunliffe Road, 1909. A 'canker' was an ulcer, usually of the mouth and lips, but the locals also called this the 'Sore-eye well'. Obviously the water was credited with healing properties and this is in keeping with its chalybeate (iron-containing) qualities. The ornate fountain was replaced by a simple stone block in 1923, but in recent years the water supply has been lost as a result of building operations across The Grove. A marble memorial bath, removed from Ben Rhydding Hydro when the hotel was demolished in 1955, is now located where the bench is situated. (M. Dixon)

8

CHURCHES, CHAPELS
AND SCHOOLS

The choir of St Margaret's Church at Ripon Cathedral, 25 July 1881. The all-male choir, twenty boys and nineteen adults, have assembled outside the west front of the cathedral for the group photograph. Some of the boys hold straw boaters as befits the fine summer's day, but others have bowlers as do many of the men. The vicar, Revd William Danks, not content with the distinction afforded by his 'dog collar', adds further to his status with a top hat. (M. Dixon)

Left: The vicar of Ilkley, Revd F. Sinker, *c.* 1910. A man of great energy and missionary zeal, Revd Sinker actively promoted outreach to the community. One Saturday evening in 1909, he toured the public houses in the town issuing invitations to men to attend the monthly men's service to be held the following day. About 800 men attended that afternoon's service at All Saints', many as a direct response to the vicar's invitation. The vicar gave an address on 'A great offer'. (T. Mutton)

Below: Ilkley Baptist Boys' Brigade, pre-1914. The two gentlemen who ran the Brigade were Mr Chedburn (left) and Mr Jarvis (right). (Kathryn Emmott)

Above: St John's Ben Rhydding church choir, October 1946.
The gentleman second from the right with the academic
hood is 'Chuff' Evans, organist and choir master, who
was the maths teacher and deputy head at the grammar
school. His nickname had an unfortunate origin; Mr Evans
was left with breathing difficulties after suffering a gas
attack during the First World War. His noisy breathing was
accompanied by a 'chuffing' sound, hence the nickname.
On the left, also looking suitably academic, is the vicar of
St John's, Revd E. Basil Alban. (A. Anning/*Ilkley Gazette*)

Right: Re-roofing All Saints' Church, *c.* 1937. Colonel
Barker, the Diocesan Surveyor, had inspected the roof some
time before and, on his advice, the vicar Canon Garland
and the church wardens decide to proceed with repair
work forthwith. The cost, estimated to be about £200, was
raised from donations by members of the congregation
and others 'who have a love for the beautiful old church'.
(C.M. Duncan)

Above: The interior of Leeds Road Congregational Hall, *c.* 1965. The hall is decorated for the annual Harvest Festival. Faced with declining numbers and increasing costs, the congregation decided, very reluctantly, to close the hall. The final service was held in May 1970. Some of the members transferred their allegiance to the Grove Congregational Church, but the great majority went nowhere. (M. Dixon)

Left: Repairs to Grove Congregational Church steeple, April 1959. (*Ilkley Gazette*)

Right: In July 1983 work was underway on converting the former Grove Congregational Church for use by Christchurch, the combined Methodist/United Reformed Church in Ilkley. The photograph has been taken looking towards the west window, which was formerly the 'front' of the sanctuary. The sanctuary is now upstairs and faces east, a new floor having been installed at about half-column height to create a lower hall and ancillary rooms. (P. Bambridge/ *Ilkley Gazette*)

Below: Ilkley Wesleyan Methodist Church choir – Wharfedale Music Festival winners, *c.* 1955. Mrs Watchhurst, the musical director/ conductor is in the middle of the front row while to her left is Mr Sydney Clark, a pillar of the Wells Road Church. (M. Dixon)

Left: The spire of Wells Road Methodist Church topples during the demolition of the building in 1970. The church was erected in 1869, when the Wesleyans, then worshipping in their humbler chapel in Skipton Road (now Nidd Vale Motors), decided that they required a more commodious and impressive place of worship. A hundred years later, however, with mounting maintenance costs and the challenge of dry rot, the members decided to demolish the church and refurbish the Assembly Hall across the road. (*Ilkley Gazette*)

Below: The former Wells Road Assembly Hall, 1974. While undergoing refurbishment, a fire caused by a contractor's blowtorch, completely gutted the roof of the hall and this had to be rebuilt at a cost of £65,000. The building was reopened in July 1975 as the Ilkley Methodist Church, whose creation followed the closure of Wells Road and Leeds Road Methodist Churches. During the refurbishment the Methodists worshipped with the Congregationalists at The Grove, thus developing relationships that led to the formation of a combined ecumenical church, Christchurch, in 1981. (*Ilkley Gazette*)

Above: The Opening Service in the newly refurbished Ilkley Methodist Church, July 1975. (M. Dixon)

Right: Leeds Road Methodist Chapel immediately before demolition, 1969. In 1858 the Primitive Methodists in Ilkley had put a deposit on land where the railway station now stands with a view to building a permanent home, but through the inactivity of the vendor the land was not conveyed and eventually a site at the corner of Wharfe View Road and Leeds Road was obtained instead. In March 1878 the chapel was opened for public worship following a procession of over 1,000 people from the fountain at the top of Brook Street down to the new building. A Sunday school building was erected in 1916. The closing activities at the Leeds Road Chapel took place in August 1969. (M. Dixon)

Leeds Road Primitive Methodist Chapel choir outing in the 1920s. The choir, with its strong bias towards sopranos, are pictured here ready to board a charabanc. Given the British climate, the fold-back canvas roof could well be needed before the day is out. The word 'charabanc' (from the French – 'coach with benches') has disappeared from modern speech. Older generations will recall that they always went on trips in a 'chara' (pronounced shara), never in a coach. (M. Dixon)

Demolition of the Leeds Road Primitive Methodist Chapel nears completion, 1969. In the background is part of the disused gas works premises (now Booth's supermarket). The site is now a car park. (P. Bambridge/*Ilkley Gazette*)

The old grammar school building, Skipton Road, *c.* 1911. The school was founded in 1607 under bequests of George Marshall and Reginald Heber. A building was finally erected and opened in 1637 under the patronage of All Saints', whose vicar was responsible for appointing the schoolmaster. Following an adverse report by the Inspector of Charities in 1867, the Church Commissioners proposed that the school should be re-established independent of the Church. In 1872 the school was closed and the pupils absorbed into the National Schools in Leeds Road awaiting the building of a new school. (Bradford Galleries and Museums)

The Ladies' High School at Tarn House, 1882. Situated at the corner of Cowpasture Road and Wheatley Road, Tarn House was designed by the prolific local architect George Smith, and erected in 1873. It was run as a girls' boarding school for some years and in 1882 a Mrs Wainwright was the principal. In 1896, with the Misses Lawrence at the helm, the school moved to larger premises in Queens Drive, into a house called Oaklands. (M. Dixon)

The senior girls of All Saints' School take part in a Japanese tableau, *c.* 1910. The young form teacher stands at the right of the group. Until 1850, Japan was largely unknown to Western cultures. The Japanese Pavilion at the World Exposition in Paris in 1867 created huge interest and there then followed a wave of Japanese influence in art and fashion throughout Europe that was to last into the twentieth century. In the early 1900s Ilkley had its own 'Jap Decorative Art Stores' on The Grove (at the corner with Wells Promenade) selling oriental fancy goods and souvenirs. (M. Dixon)

Young girls from All Saints' pose in their white dresses while holding coloured ribbons, *c.* 1910. The Ribbon Dance was one of the better known English country dances taught at school. The tradition of country dancing was maintained in our junior schools as a matter of course. From 1921 to 1931 there was a flourishing section of the Wharfedale Festival in which local schools and groups regularly competed. So successful was this activity that a separate festival was held in 1930 and 1931. Apart from the Ribbon Dance, schoolchildren performed the Black Nag, Rufty Tufty and the Yorkshire Straight Sword Dance among many others. (M. Dixon)

Heathfield School, Westwood Drive, *c.* 1911. One of Ilkley's numerous small private schools. After one month of the new school year, a girl writes; 'Everything has changed here. I am in the 5th form, so Kathleen, Minnie and Co., are 6th formers!!! Quite grown up. We are having a lovely time here. I am in the top bedroom (with 'X' marking the windows), Minnie, Gladys, Marjorie, Magdelaine, a new girl Kath and myself. We have such fun.' (M. Dixon)

The assembly hall at Heathfield School, *c.* 1911. This room, and the number of chairs, gives a clear idea of the size and limited facilities of this private school. The ethos of the school is indicated by the 'uplifting' verses on the wall. One reads: 'Like as a star that maketh not haste, That taketh not rest, Be each one fulfilling His God-given Best.' The verse was reproduced in *Stray thoughts for Girls* by Lucy Soulsby (1903), a book dedicated to 'girls at the awkward age'. (M. Dixon)

Pupils at Heathfield School take part in an open-air rendition of *As You Like It, c.* 1910. The all-girl cast have taken on the roles of Touchstone, the Duke Senior (complete with generous facial hair), courtiers, shepherds and goat-herds, as well as the damsels in distress. No additional scenery has been required to capture the feel of the Forest of Ardennes. Heathfield closed in 1942 and later became Moorland House School for delinquent boys. (M. Dixon)

A class of pupils at the Church of England Infants' School ('Bottom School'), Leeds Road, *c.* 1930. Behind the railings are allotments that extend to Bath Street. The small hut in the background belonged to Robert Haxby, a boot and shoe repairer. In more recent years it was occupied by the Ilkley Model Centre, but has now been demolished (along with the 'National Schools' building) to make way for a housing development. (Betty Burton)

Class IV at Ben Rhydding Council School, *c.* 1932. This was an all-age school, taking pupils from five to fourteen years of age, under the control of the old West Riding Education Committee. After the war it became Ilkley Secondary Modern School and, in recent years, Bolling Road (now Ben Rhydding) First School. (Win Porritt)

Ilkley Grammar School and the headmaster's house, *c.* 1901. The present building was opened in 1893 as a grammar school for day boys and boarders. It was greatly enlarged within five years by the addition of laboratories and specialist rooms. The school continued to grow in numbers and amenities in the 1930s. In 1961 a new building scheme was commenced that greatly increased its capacity. (M. Dixon)

One of the art rooms at Ilkley Grammar School, *c*. 1901. (M. Dixon)

Ilkley Grammar School sports day, 1948. The sports fields occupied land on Valley Drive where the International Wool Secretariat (now Optident) was later built. The long-jumper is Eric Sutton, who played rugby for Ilkley and Otley before turning professional and playing rugby league for Bradford Northern. (P.A. Thornton)

Students at Ilkley Grammar School perform *Julius Caesar*, 1956. One reviewer said of the production: 'It is certainly a fine play, and in many ways a good choice, having several main characters of varying importance and ample opportunity for others in a large supporting cast. In a mixed school, however, one feels that it might have been wiser to choose a play in which both sexes are more evenly represented. As it was, the girls were neglected, being required only for two minor parts, while the boys were called upon to supply more talent than they could produce.' The grammar school first admitted girls in 1939. (M. Dixon)

Ilkley Grammar School pupils on top of Ilkley Moor, 1953. In recognition of the Queen's Coronation, it was decided that a summit cairn should be built at the highest point of the moor visible from the main entrance of the Grammar School. On the way up, the students were encouraged to pick up a stone to add to the pile at the top. Before creating the cairn, a hole was dug and a box containing a copy of the school magazine, a school cap and other mementoes were buried before covering it with the pile of stones. The cairn still stands today. (M. Dixon)

Boys from Ilkley Secondary Modern School (on Bolling Road) working in their allotments behind the school, 1962. The pupils could buy a small white turnip for a penny; these were eaten raw at break-time, and provided 'a delicious cheap snack' according to one former student. (*Ilkley Gazette*)

Oaklands School Hockey Festival, March 1964. Oaklands was one of Ilkley's more successful and durable private schools. This well-attended gathering of hockey players was one of the last sporting occasions held at Oaklands, for the school closed in 1965 following the death of the headmaster, Mr Saville. (N.R. Thompson/*Ilkley Gazette*)

9

AROUND THE TOWN
– A MISCELLANY

The top of Wells Road, *c.* 1885. In the foreground Hainsworth's pond is shown in its original form. On the right is Wells Terrace while across Crossbeck Road are Moor Cottage and the houses comprising South View. The houses of West View run down the hill – the view, unlike today, unobstructed by trees! To the left are the Royal Hotel, built in 1871 and demolished in 1962 to make way for Wells Court, and the side of Linndale, one of a pair of private houses built in 1871. (G. Burton)

'Ilkley from the Moor', *c.* 1915. This photograph was taken from above the junction of Hangingstone Road and Maxwell Road. The most prominent buildings are, from left to right: the Stoneylea Hotel (demolished), the Grammar School, Greystones, Burnside (demolished) and Wharfedale (now Moorfield) School. (M. Dixon)

Moorlands Hydro and Boarding Establishment, *c.* 1910. Moorlands was situated in Crossbeck Road, next to the Craiglands Hotel. A well-known Ilkley character, Lister Robinson, was the proprietor. After the First World War, the hotel became a private residence occupied by William Robinson and his family. In the 1950s the hotel was purchased by the owners of Craiglands, who demolished the building to provide additional car-parking space. Craiglands Park now occupies the site. (M. Dixon)

Demolition of the Royal Hotel commences, 1962. The 'Royal' was a popular place for dining out and there were dances on a Saturday night. At the right-hand side, in Wells Road, there was a separate entrance into the tap-room. (M. Dixon)

The Ilkley Moor Hotel in Skipton Road immediately after a fire, July 1968. The fire broke out in the lounge of the hotel in the early hours of Tuesday 30 July, and spread rapidly once it reached the main staircase. The upper floors were engulfed in flames and four people were killed: two guests – a farmer from Lancashire and his son – and two members of staff. The damage was so severe that the hotel had to be demolished shortly afterwards. (P.A. Thornton)

Thomas Richardson, cobbler, *c.* 1905. Mr Richardson moved his boot and shoe repair shop to The Grove after his original shop in Brook Street had been demolished. Around 1900, however, he 'down-sized' to this hut in South Hawksworth Street. Over to the left are the glass-houses of the Brook Street Nurseries. (G. Burton)

The north-west corner of the central car park, *c.* 1968. The white building is Lawson's Builders and Plumbers premises. The house at the right belongs to Mr and Mrs Lawson while next door is Roy Cunliffe's motorcycle shop and on the extreme right is the side of the West Yorkshire bus depot. One of Ilkley's most famous sons is the gardener and television personality Alan Titchmarsh. His father (also Alan) was in charge of the plumbing department at Lawson's. (*Ilkley Gazette*)

Moving houses, Railway Road, *c.* 1885. This row of houses (then called Wilmot Street) adjoined Wilmot House – the tall house at the end with the prominent gable – before being removed to make way for the new lines needed for the extension of the railway from Ilkley to Skipton in 1886. Wilmot House survived intact, as the new Railway Road was angled around it. The short terrace also survived after a fashion, because the houses were carefully dismantled and re-erected on the north side of Leeds Road between Wharfe View Road and Weston Road. It is difficult now, however, to identify the houses as there has been extensive conversion into shops in this area. (Win Porritt)

The staff of Thirkell's shop, Railway Road, 1986. Elaine Naylor, Michael and Zena Bower, Frank Williamson and Edna Pocklington pose for the camera just before the shop's closure in 1986. Thirkell's was a widely renowned pork pie shop. It was claimed that Thirkell's pies were made according to a secret recipe; this seems unlikely but their special quality was difficult to reproduce. (P. Bambridge/*Ilkley Gazette*)

Church Street, *c.* 1900. (G. Burton)

The 'Charity Hole', Church Street, 1893. The porch of the old vicarage served as a dispensary where the curate, George Fenton, gave out simple remedies in the 1820s and '30s – hence 't'old charity 'ole'. The noticeboard belongs to the Great Northern Railway and displays train timetables and notices of excursions, while inside the doorway there are posters about the Local Board election and a story in the *Ilkley Gazette* about 'Oswald Lister and the Local Board'. (G. Burton)

Above: The top of Bridge Lane, 1953. The Hillman/Commer pick-up belongs to Glover's Garage. Note Lister's Arms Hotel on the right, and on the left the antique shop that was soon to become the Box Tree Restaurant. Beyond the public bar of the hotel is the railway bridge over Cunliffe Road. (A. Anning/*Ilkley Gazette*)

Right: Shops in Wells Road at the junction with Chantry Drive, *c.* 1910. The Ilkley Wells Café had been recently established by Messrs Clarkson and Holgate. It was destined to remain a café for many years thereafter. The next-door premises belonged to Jesse Bontoft, 'artist and photographer', who recorded the Ilkley scene for more than forty years from the 1880s onwards. Originally, his shop-cum-studio was in Brook Street but this was demolished in the 1890s. (Lydia Pettit)

The top of Church Street in the 1950s. The Wheatsheaf Hotel, on the left, was tied to Bentley's Brewery of Rotherham (hence BYB – Bentley's Yorkshire Beers) and was demolished in 1959. The site was incorporated into the gardens around All Saints' Church. Beyond is the Star Inn and Fox's celebrated pie shop. George Fox had two Daimler vans fitted out as 'travelling shops' and these went up and down the Dales visiting farms and villages to sell pork pies, bacon, hams and preserved meats. On the right of Church Street are Swales' chemist shop and beyond a bakery belonging to the Misses Kemp. (G. Burton)

Margaret and Basil Easby, *c.* 1970. Easby's clothing (and school uniform) shop in Leeds Road was founded by Basil's father, a stern disciplinarian who had a no-nonsense attitude to selling school uniforms. Eric Spencer was an employee and at the end of the Second World War, Eric was responsible for measuring up the convalescing soldiers at the Middleton Sanatorium for their 'de-mob' suits. These were supplied by Easby's under a Ministry of Defence contract. (M. Dixon)

David Lishman's butchers shop, 25 Leeds Road, 1991. Lishman's has expanded a great deal in recent years and now occupies what were originally three adjacent shops. Interestingly, No. 23 was a butcher's shop in the 1920s and '30s belonging to Thomas Shearsmith, but he appears to have moved to the shop next door prior to selling the business to Percy Driver soon after the war. David Lishman took over the lease from Mr Driver in 1986. (A.M. Grunwell)

The manager's house, Ilkley Gas Works, 1969. Besides producing town gas, the gas works sold coke (the residue after making gas from coal) both to fuel merchants and to the public. The merchant's lorries used the weighbridge near the manager's house, but the public bought it by the bagful. You had to provide your own sacks and the full bags had to be carried home. This was achieved using old prams, wheelbarrows and 'bogeys', as home-made go-carts were known in those days. (P. Bambridge/*Ilkley Gazette*)

The public library, Sedbergh Buildings and Tower Buildings from Station Road, 1966. Tower Buildings were erected in 1874 for Robinson & Sons, makers of the famous 'Ilkley Couch'. During excavation of the foundations, several funerary urns and a chamber containing ornaments, rings and bracelets thought to be of Roman origin, were uncovered. The Cowpasture Road side of the building was occupied by shops, including the successors to Robinson's furniture business – Hartley & Sons. The buildings were demolished in 1970 and replaced by Leconfield House. (P.A. Thornton)

Tower Buildings just before demolition, c. 1970. This view from Springs Terrace shows three houses – separate from the shops that occupy the Cowpasture Road aspect, the one on the right was occupied by Mr Douglas Hatch who was in charge of the Ilkley bathing pool during the 1940s and '50s. (P. Bambridge/*Ilkley Gazette*)

Middelton Park from the foot of Langbar Road, *c.* 1905. The house in the middle distance is Oak Ghyll, built in 1900 and the first of a series of impressive villas to appear in Middleton. In the 1960s it was used as a convalescent home but after its sale in 1970, was converted into apartments. (M. Dixon)

A Victorian pillar box at the corner of Middleton Avenue and Denton Road, 1951. Pillar boxes were first introduced to the Channel Islands in 1852 and a year later in mainland Britain. They were initially rectangular but between 1866 and 1879 the hexagonal 'Penfold' became the standard design and at first were painted sage green. It was not until 1874 that they became the familiar red. Very few of these hexagonal boxes remain in use today, possibly only two or three in the country. Before this box was installed at Ilkley, it stood at the foot of Leeds Road, Bradford, for many years. (C.M. Duncan)

'Golf ground', Ben Rhydding Hydro, 1885. As enthusiasm for the 'water-cure' waned, the hotel promoted and developed its other sporting facilities including its tennis courts and croquet lawns, and by around 1885 a nine-hole golf course. During the early twentieth century Ben Rhydding advertised itself as a golf-hotel, but it was not a great success. The hotel closed after the Second World War. With the demise of the Ilkley Moor Golf Club, a number of golf enthusiasts met at the Wheatley Hotel and established the Ben Rhydding Golf Club in 1947. (Ilkley Public Library)

Duell's tea rooms, Ben Rhydding, c. 1910. This distinctive building was erected as a toll-house on the Otley–Skipton turnpike. In the Victorian period it became a farmhouse occupied by the Duell family, and it was Thomas Duell who created the tea rooms in the early 1900s. In 1934 the building and surrounding land was the subject of a compulsory purchase in order to carry out road-widening and the house was demolished. In 1936 a garage was built on the adjacent land and this later became Ross Brothers' car showroom and garage. (Betty Burton)

Wright's butchers shop, *c.* 1912. Mr George Wright's shop at 3 Bolling Road, Ben Rhydding, decked out for Christmas. (P.A. Thornton)

A view of Bolling Road and Ben Rhydding shops looking east, *c.* 1935. The shops comprise Ellis Beanlands, grocer at No. 1; Edwin Woodhouse, greengrocer at 3; Frank Dufton, pastrycook at 5; Fred Myers & Son, plumbers at 9; Sam Woodcock, butcher at 11; Charles Carter, painter and decorator at 13; John Sykes, grocer at 15; and a sub-branch of the Midland Bank at 17. (P.A. Thornton)

Opposite above: On the old Nesfield Road, *c.* 1900. The original road to Nesfield started from a point just beyond the Old Bridge and ran along the bank of the river before swinging north to approach the golf club 'pavilion' as Common Holme Lane. (G. Burton)

Opposite below: Rounding up stray sheep, 1958. At the beginning of September 1958, the Council launched an operation to round up stray sheep wandering around the streets and gardens of the town. On the first day, 115 sheep and lambs had been gathered and impounded. Here a small flock has been collected on Denton Road near the Suspension Bridge. (A. Anning/*Ilkley Gazette*)

The view over Ilkley from the terrace of the Moorlands Hydro in Crossbeck Road, *c.* 1900. The houses on the left are those of Mount Pleasant. (M. Dixon)

Hangingstone Road and the Cow and Calf Rocks from the Highfield Hotel (now the Cow and Calf Hotel), *c.* 1900. (M. Dixon)

Other titles published by The History Press

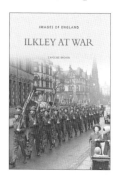

Ilkley at War
CAROLINE BROWN

This fascinating book looks at how Ilkley, Burley and Menton adapted to the many changing circumstances brought about by the war including the arrival of evacuees and European refugees, gas masks and rationing, Government initiatives like 'Holidays at Home', War Savings and the Home Guard. This book will be a nostalgic trip for those that lived through the war years and a revelation for those that didn't.

978 0 7524 4191 7

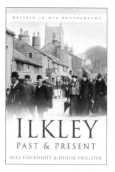

Ilkley Past & Present
ALEX COCKSHOTT & DENISE SHILLITOE

With the help of old photographs, this book traces the history of Ilkley from being a small town to a place of tourist attraction. Referred to in the Domesday Book, it was a small agricultural village for centuries; all this changed when the potential of the local waters was realised in the eighteenth century, and Ilkley became known as a spa.

978 0 7509 3922 5

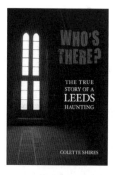

Who's There? The True Story of a Leeds Haunting
COLETTE SHIRES

When the Shires family heard what sounded like a baby crying in their new house, they had no idea that it was the beginning of a terrifying haunting that would last for more than thirty years, and follow them across the city. This is their story.

978 0 7524 4808 4

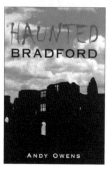

Haunted Bradford
ANDY OWENS

Drawing on historical and contemporary sources, including the hitherto unpublished findings of the Haunted Yorkshire Psychical Research team, this book unearths a chilling range of supernatural phenomena. From the spectre with a seat reserved at The Priestly Theatre to the pale-faced lady of the White Swan Inn, the spirit of Branwell Brontë and 'Charlie', the invisible cleaner who helps staff at City Hall, all the phantom residents of the city are recorded here.

978 0 7524 4482 6

Visit our website and discover thousands of other History Press books.

www.thehistorypress.co.uk